The Beyoncé Phenomenon

The Beyoncé Phenomenon

Fiona Sterling

Contents

1

Disclaimer

The content in this book is intended for informational and entertainment purposes only. While every effort has been made to ensure the accuracy of the information presented, the author and publisher make no representations or warranties of any kind, express or implied, about the completeness, accuracy, reliability, suitability, or availability with respect to the content of this book.

The views and opinions expressed in this book are those of the author and do not necessarily reflect the official policy or position of any individual, company, or organization mentioned. Any resemblance to actual persons, living or dead, or actual events is purely coincidental.

This book is not intended to defame, libel, or slander any person, company, or organization. All references to individuals, companies, products, and brands are for illustrative purposes only, and no affiliation with or endorsement by them is intended or implied.

The author and publisher disclaim any responsibility for any actions or outcomes resulting from the application of information contained in this book. Readers should seek professional advice or conduct their own research when making decisions based on the content provided.

All rights reserved. No part of this book may be reproduced, distributed, or transmitted in any form or by any means, including photocopying, recording, or other electronic or mechanical methods, without the prior written permission of the author, except in the case of brief quotations embodied in critical reviews and certain other non-commercial uses permitted by copyright law.

2

Introduction

In the modernity of the American music industry, vantage is worth a great deal. The invaluable commodity of historical significance gives Beyoncé an important advantage as a modern artist. It's difficult to imagine that there was ever a time when she was not acknowledged as an American treasure or a member of the Vice President's family when clips of her ad-libs went viral. For many, Beyoncé is Queen Bey, and no one else will be compared to her. Given the sour yet lucrative enterprise of marketing presidential merchandise, Beyoncé's position as a visible Black icon is all the more striking.

Beyoncé's path towards world domination began in a small community in Houston. From her earliest days in Destiny's Child to her ascent as a solo artist, Beyoncé's evolution as an artist and woman has been synonymous with personal growth and going beyond personal boundaries and limitations—and the history of our time. In order to give readers a better understanding of the woman and artist Beyoncé, each subsequent chapter will guide readers through the various stages of her artistic development, detailing her unique artistry and the extent of her impact. In doing so, I hope to expose a bard from the ghetto silenced by commercial media and defend her innovative accomplishments in the shadow of pop music.

3

Chapter 1: The Rise of Destiny's Child

Destiny's Child was never anything other than Beyoncé Knowles's group. Formed by her father in 1992 with classmates LaTavia Robertson and Kelly Rowland, Destiny's Child was meant to be a female counterpart to the teenage hip-hop group of which Beyoncé's first cousin was a member. As the two girls had just turned 9, it would be a few years before Destiny's Child would be in a position to market themselves as such. Beyoncé often claimed to be the main songwriter and sole producer within the group, controlling Destiny's Child like a diva.

The group's first album flopped. But then, it seems their fans didn't care about the group as much as they cared about Destiny's Child and, to be even more specific, about Beyoncé. Her father Mathew Knowles, under somewhat financial pressure to do so, signed on for the show after he began to understand the buzz surrounding his daughter. And the show put a well-known recording contract with Elektra Records on the table. Only days after the MTV special aired, Destiny's Child signed with Columbia Records, included. During that time, Tymalone Box was released and brought a string of top ten singles and won a few Teen Choice Awards. Kelly and LaTavia weren't the only ones who felt that the band's success was pleasurable to Beyoncé and Beyoncé only. Back in '97, Beyoncé explained the meaning of the group's song with some humblebraggin': "We can help other people to be crazy in love with themselves."

Formation of the Group

Destiny's Child, a girl band synonymous with female empowerment, mega hits, and truly iconic stage costumes, formed in Houston, Texas in 1990. The group members were preteens and teenagers at the time of their formation and skyrocketed to superstardom, often embodying the idea of the American dream through their music. Their music reflected the unique combination of entertainment's form of confessional narrative and a more accurate reflection of how women navigate personal and professional relationships in a neoliberal world.

In fact, before the success of making their way through talent shows and showcase gigs, or the power of the bootylicious back catalog, there was just a small group of Catholic backyard friends from the Southeast area of Houston whose mothers went to church together and wanted their daughters to sing. The true reason that Destiny's Child is so special is not their flame-haired center-partings or their matching silver PVC two-pieces, but the fact that they seamlessly formed and reformed to keep up with the latest pop incarnation of Destiny's Child. It would be amiss to detach their late-nineties debut from the post-millennial pop supernova of Beyoncé's solo debut.

Like so many girl group origin stories, the roots of Destiny's Child can be traced back to the aspirations of ancestors long before their children even thought of the Supremes or the Ronettes. When Beyoncé and Kelly made their first television appearance on "Star Search" in 1992, singing an a cappella rendition of John Lennon's

"Imagine," the girls introduced themselves as "the Singing Sisters." Managed initially by Beyoncé's father, Mathew Knowles, the group churned through several incarnations until they finally received some local radio attention with their song "No, No, No." The track made its way to recording artist Wyclef Jean and was subsequently given a remix, which caught the eye of Columbia Records' then-president Don Welorick. Thus, Destiny's Child was successfully formed.

Early Successes

In 1997, Destiny's Child - the girl group that would later help cement Beyoncé's iconic status - was signed to Elektra Records. With this connection, Beyoncé and Kelly's parents managed to get them in front of executives at both Sony and Death Row Records. By the following year, the various record labels the group was housed under were at odds, and in spite of soon having a major deal with Sony Music, Combs was dropped as their manager. With Sony no longer interested in working with Destiny's Child and Combs out of the picture, Knowles' father sought out the manager of Wyclef Jean, who got the group signed to a deal with Columbia.

In 1998, Destiny's Child released their eponymous debut album, a 16-track record of up-tempo funk and mid-tempo R&B mixed with occasional ballads like "With Me" and "Second Nature". Despite having released instrumentals for the self-titled album two years prior with R&B diva, Christina Aguilera, indie label Peoplesound Records found themselves in a battle for legality after Beyoncé and Christaun "Stina" McCrimmon recorded the sixteen furthermore songs with Destiny's Child. The "chains of custody" were considered secure and valid as the Brit claimed that the contract signed with Knowles and "Denzil" described it as the lawful procedure to obtain the records, and the signing was "conducted in an orderly way." The Beyoncé Adorée records were produced with the help of Rob Fusari.

4

Chapter 2: Beyoncé's Solo Career Begins

That IEEE brought out a special report to celebrate and "examine the evolution, achievements, and impact of women in engineering over the last several decades" indicates the urgency of the gender balance problem in engineering. What better role model could the IEEE find than Beyoncé Knowles, the Las Vegas native who is the most Grammy-nominated woman and second-most Grammy-awarded woman in history and whom Vogue once declared "the best entertainer of our generation"? "Cultural studies has often pointed to popular music, celebrities, and performed stardom as within a feminine wheelhouse, but more than just a catchall site of girlish practice, superstars themselves are making millions more than the men in their field evident at their final tours and final paychecks," Sarah Banet-Weiser explained. "Thanks to stylized marketing, public relations, new possibilities of communication technologies, and merchandising, women are publicized through their bodies as people to watch."

This report aims to look at a specific star and to map through a number of constructs the audience's relation to Beyoncé. It will start by delving deeply into her same-named fifth album because it mirrors Beyoncé's self-described most prolific time in the music studio as a solo artist. Then a brief look at her career with Destiny's Child will help to show Beyoncé as she began to take control of her own career. A look at her life offstage, including her family, business, and social work, illustrates how she has created parallel roles as a mother, celebrity, and business magnate. The report will finish by looking at Walkers, a classroom as Beyoncé's business, music, or perceptions layer over each other as a form of cultural privilege.

Dangerously in Love Album

Beyoncé chose the release date for her solo debut to coincide with the band's anniversary, suggesting a subtler approach to both her individual career and Wang. The nine days that separate the two occasions give an idea of the different strategies. By celebrating 7 June, Beyoncé reaffirms her loyalty to the past, addressing herself to the most attentive, and potentially older, fans who remember those years, and taking advantage of the interest that Destiny's Child, among the first girl bands to break, continues to attract with their own singles - even after their breakup. The first joint biography of the three, written by Kelly Price and published in 2002, is aimed at teenagers, the largest slice of their supporters, who relate to their experience as a potential model.

Released on 22 June (the first track, "Crazy in Love", leaked in advance of the single - just two days after the tenth anniversary), her first solos feature the sound of a mature, complete, unconventional vocal and personal artist. Beyoncé has also unveiled the secret of her debut single. If she didn't want to talk about her marriage to Jay-Z, she told MTV, "it is the craziness that brings us together". It can be difficult to keep weight in check, you cannot get involved in sentimental relationships, hearts break after a moment of fusion, and one dance is enough to fall in love and be crazy - in the matter, as in feeling. Written by one of the two U.K. rappers, "Crazy in Love" is a passionate, catchy, powerful - and peculiarly retro - demonstration. The beat is a sample of a "You Can't Sit Down" of the 1960s, the voices are distorted borrowed from the hip-hop of the late Bossy. Domination, remixed so they sound like a tangle of lines played vintage year.

Crazy in Love Single

Watching Beyoncé open with "Crazy in Love" while flames from the stage rise around her, flamenco influences in her music and the music video, seeing her dance at a football game, the group of artists with whom she collaborates, her show across the world where she invites Jay-Z to the stage and kisses him, or her strict volume of fans—5.3 million expected ticket sales across 32 shows—suggests this Grammy-winning and chart-topping single will always be near to the writer.

Following Destiny's Child's 2001 release Survivor, Beyoncé turned her focus to recording her first full-length album Dangerously in Love. With the help from producer Rich Harrison, the Bee Gees' "Are You My Woman (Tell Me So)" sample, and rapper Jay-Z who was a long-time friend and now collaborator, the party-like single "Crazy in Love" was put together.

Released in May of 2003, Billboard Weekly describes the single as an "aphrodisiac before the body's even gotten into motion." A month later, the third single featuring Jay-Z hit the No. 1 spot on Billboard's Hot 100 and the Billboard Hot R&B/Hip-Hop Singles chart by leaping from No. 14. In response to the single's rapidly climbing charts, journalist Jeff Vrabel wrote, "Crazy in Love," "her first true, solo, non-soundtrack single, is a scorcher." Use of connatural vocal arrangers, strong bass lines, and sexy brass riffs lay the groundwork for Beyoncé to begin her solo career. Since the single's release, Alexandra Topping has reported, "A string of singles debuted at number one in the US, while albums and singles shifted by the bucketload everywhere else, not just for her, but for Destiny's Child, so swiftly did she dominate her audience and also the Billboard charts.

5

Chapter 3: Evolution of Beyoncé's Sound

In Destiny's Child, and for the first few years of her solo career, Beyoncé's music was rooted in classic 90's R&B. Throughout her career, Beyoncé has worked with the most influential music producers in the business, and her song output of over 300 songs reflects the myriad of styles and songs for which she is known. Rudy Blanco, who played with Destiny's Child, testified to this, "Beyoncé would write these classic 90's throwback R&B ballads.

Subsequent to Solo Star, Beyoncé's adult sound emerged on the 2003 album Dangerously In Love, which gave her her first international hit, "Crazy In Love," and has a more pop sound - in part because most of the album was co-produced by Rich Harrison, who was responsible for "Crazy In Love." Notably, Sean Garrett wrote five of the songs along with the vocals, and Jin Choi is listed as an arranger on the song. In this album, she abandoned the more urban, hip-hop sound of Destiny's Child of the early 2000s and Al, and began to explore a pop sound. Beyoncé herself recognized her sonic evolution when she was all over TV in 2003. 2003 was also the year she starred in the singing-slash-stripping scenes in The Fighting Temptations, which led to her role in Dreamgirls a few years later. "I think my vocals have grown, and I think my tastes in music and experimenting with all the different sounds [has too]," she said. By the time of the premiere of her breakout film, Dreamgirls, in 2006, Beyoncé was ready to flex her songwriting skills.

B'Day Album

The release of B'Day affirmed Beyoncé's position as one of music's most powerful women. After announcing an April 2006 release for the edgy new material, the date of her birthday, Beyoncé did not wander and cozy up to an embrace of self-immensely disinterested fans. Instead, she plugged in and programmed the festivities. Five solo tours, a brief reuniting with her Destiny's Child comrades, over three dozen music videos, one major film presence in the Academy Award-winning Dreamgirls, marriage (at last) to hip-hop mogul Jay-Z, and a wealth of endorsement and philanthropy work later, for those willing to listen, Beyoncé still has plenty to say.

Between itself and her 2003 Dangerously in Love debut, the music industry had discovered Beyoncé was more than a pretty alto in the muscular powerhouse pop-R&B quartet Destiny's Child. The star that shook her bootylicious hip-hop translating resolution washed, the anti-materialistic daddy's girl defending women's worth walked, and the classy woman-on-top let down her know-the-facts tumble and soar on "Cater 2 U," "Irreplaceable," and "Deja Vu" respectively. Her genuine vulnerability let its hair down (vocal or metaphorical) on ballads like "Me, Myself and I," "Dangerously in Love," and "Speechless," but it was definitely the power pair of bolly-R&B headbangers "Crazy in Love" and "Baby Boy" that solidified independence.

Riding out the last two years and counting on her timetable of experience since Destiny, released in 1998, Beyoncé finally gets back at the life through a continuum preceded by her innate relationship to it. Her second solo release, tentatively titled B'Day, is bound to bring with it a fresh aesthetic of (self-)discovery, freedom, and love. It's really an answer album of sorts. Sure, she was fumbling and crumbling with depression (as much as sleep deprivation, you'd think), the godly presence of Diana Ross, and co-leads Jennifer Hudson and Jamie Foxx playing up for the time, but in the end, success was the love from an audience to cast as their personal poster child and one of the top five swell voices of the tortured soul (and those proud to sing them).

Sasha Fierce Alter Ego

The double-disc album "I Am ... Sasha Fierce" was the third studio album released by Beyoncé. Described by Beyoncé as being "either side of who I am," the Sasha Fierce alter ego was more sensual, more aggressive, and more outspoken, while Beyoncé was more inside out and more reflective. For Beyoncé, the creation of an alter ego was nothing new. From B'Day's "Upgrade U", "I was there like it was me who was chilling with my friends, me who was cautious about everything. I thought that the Beyoncé I wanted to be was surpassing me in every way. There wasn't a thing that I couldn't do." According to Serrano, Beyoncé's interest in creating an alter ego began with a trip to see the play Dreamgirls at a young age, the concept of the duality of one's nature appealing to her. She later based her portrayal of Deena on the duality of her nature.

Sasha Fierce would go on to have a significant impact on Beyoncé's work, from the decision to become involved in the creation of her stage costumes to her performances. "Single Ladies", which is considered one of Beyoncé's signature songs, is in fact sung by Sasha Fierce, who has a fire and an aggression that is not present in the reserved Beyoncé. Serrano wrote, "In a sense, it's easy for someone to pour their guts out about a concept if they're also given the ability to pretend that it isn't them who's doing the pouring. The fact of the matter is that Beyoncé is only one section of a Venn diagram of a person she's built." An important influence in Beyoncé's life was the idea of alter ego as a motivator for her music. While this revelation of her alter ego has largely been critiqued by critics, Beyoncé says that it gave the music more emotional depth.

6

Chapter 4: Impact of Beyoncé's Feminism

Say Beyoncé's name in any social circle, and the discussion about race, gender, and sexuality is inevitable. How do we begin unpacking what Beyoncé has contributed to the conversation surrounding women's equality in the United States? Kelly Rowland, Beyoncé's friend for twenty plus years and former Destiny's Child bandmate, writes, "Beyoncé is a goddess, not because she is good at what she does, or because she looks a certain way. No! Beyoncé is a goddess because she's a feminist. Beyoncé is a feminist because she believes in equal opportunity for her son and daughter. Beyoncé is a feminist because she hears and respects voices that speak to the important issues of women around the world."

While there is truth within Rowland's statement, there are characteristics of Beyoncé's personal brand of feminism that should accompany it. Beyoncé's public statement of feminism was a tool to increase her fan base when it became the popular work of the time. However, she represents women with power and money. Women who have the ability to let their feminism do the work while they sit back and relax. While this type of feminist helps to progress the movement, the focus of this chapter will not be directed to women like a young Beyoncé. This chapter will not discuss Beyoncé's demonization of feminists who do not subscribe to her lifestyle but appreciate her name as a marketing tactic. This chapter is full of people like Associate Professor Jillian Hernandez, an Afro-Latina professor who states, "I need for feminism to move beyond the homogeneous vision of mainstream white women, effectively silencing the 'real feminist' struggle, and women of color once and for all." Instead, we will look at the dichotomy that Beyoncé both promotes and dismantles.

Formation Single

Written by Beyoncé, Michael L. Williams II, and Khalif Brown - professionally known as Mike WiLL Made-It - the song "Formation" was released digitally as a single on February 6, 2016. It then became part of the "Lemonade" album. This provocative and revolutionary song was instantly described as an explicit "black power anthem". The video that accompanied the song premiered on YouTube one day before the U.S. The video is part of practices employed by singer-songwriters like Bruce Springsteen or Prince, where the songs are accompanied by a video that gives them "a broader political canvas, a wider humanity, far beyond the shopworn clichés of the commercial marketplace".

Beyoncé's "Formation" is a feminist anthem, but also a song about women's empowerment. It is about self-worth and independence. The rhythm is contagious and the beat is uplifting; it has become an anthem for numerous demonstrations. "Formation" is a song about race and racial identity. It is a critique of racial inequities, police brutality, and the basic inequities of living in a Black body. It does this by celebrating pop-cultural touchstones of African American identity. Beyoncé's song is an example of pop music of its moment, combining "gritty Southern trap, cackling brass, and yelling hip-hop". The song has highly racialized lyrics with one specific set of marks identifying black people: her father was from "Alabama, my momma was from Louisiana, you mix that Negro with a Creole, make a Texas bamma". One of the images accompanying the release of the song is a cropped image of a "bedazzled afro pick". "Formation" opens with the slow, heavy beat of New Orleans Bounce.

Lemonade Visual Album

The 2016 visual album Lemonade has had several different themes attributed to it, including infidelity, feminism, and black womanhood and Southern heritage in the United States. These, combined with the visual narrative set up in the videos, particularly concerned with the visual motifs and imagery of the fashion and the symbolism to the African diaspora, have allowed Lemonade to become a 'cultural conversation' made visual. This visual album has taken on a strong resonance with Americans discussing and exploring issues of race, gender, and the black American experience. A study from Nielsen found that as of 2018, white American adults are ranked the highest consumers of R&B/hip-hop music in the country, thus indicating a predominantly white audience. This means much of the cultural discussion on Lemonade is filtered through this demographic.

Reactions and receptions to Lemonade: the eruption of "Formation"

After the release, Lemonade became the best-selling album of 2016, certified double-platinum in the United States and has over 80 awards and nominations associated. Like 4 however, Lemonade is in the Top 100 best albums of the 21st century listed by Rolling Stone magazine at number 26. Originally exclusive to Tidal, the streaming service purchased by Jay-Z in mid-2015, Lemonade became more widely purchased at music retail outlets in mid-April 2016 and released in audio form shortly after on iTunes. The album acted as a force and platform not only as an exploration of "Beyoncé: the artist" and "Beyoncé: the woman" but also Jay-Z's infidelities added a level of reality and vulnerability many Americans could relate to.

7

Chapter 5: Business Ventures and Philanthropy

This chapter outlines the artist's entrepreneurial skills, focusing on her large investments in brands and creative companies, such as Ivy Park, Parkwood Production, her fragrance Heat, and Halls Soda. The singer has a net worth of more than $7 billion and, beyond her music and acting career, her knowledge in business is highly profitable. Moreover, in her recent projects, Beyoncé has imbued these with a philanthropic touch to invest in black enterprises and collaborators; some of the most well-known of these initiatives are her album Lemonade, her film Black Is King, and the Homecoming Scholarship Program. The chapter also discusses Beyoncé's public-formula philanthropy in the spheres of HIV/AIDS, breast cancer, and women's health.

However, one of the most important issues to point out is that black feminists are wary of praising everything Beyoncé does because she uses in her favor "complicities, ambiguities, intersectional blamelessness, and respectability" to sell herself as a "positive role model." She is seen by "black feminists with an enlivened interest in girlhood... [as] a fame-worthy corporate superstar" who occasionally uses her philanthropy and publicly inflected feminism "to authorize the valuable work done behind the scenes by black girls and women." In short, black feminists warn that we are following a facile and Western reading of feminist solidarity and failing to pay attention to the real issues underlying the commodification of girls' bodies and the imposition of white "modernity and propriety."

Ivy Park Clothing Line

Beyoncé Knowles-Carter, the pop singer, extends her brand and finds a new outlet for expressing her creative vision. Beyoncé co-owns the clothing line with her business partner, the CEO of Topshop. Ivy Park was sold at Topshop stores and in other department stores around the world as part of a collaboration that made her a significant member of the Topshop team.

Fashion, entertainment, and empowerment are interlinked in a way that they were not in previous times. Clothing lines created by entertainers, models, actors (some of whom moonlight as musicians), and other pop figures are part of this expanding business. Having a business, and at times having a specific kind of business, has become an intrinsic feature of a megastar's appeal. As a global superstar, Beyoncé takes on various professional roles as an entrepreneur. While creating music and performing around the world brings her significant profit, she is also a businesswoman. She and her father co-created House of Deréon, a mid-range clothing line for the junior market. House of Deréon launched with very strong sales. Even in the early 2000s, the clothing did really well at upscale department stores. Doctor Robert Kleiner, who helped Deréon launch, said in an interview that "we did $3,000,000 in 45 minutes" at a trunk show in Japan. Beyoncé was the inspiration behind the singer's fashion line. She described the brand as "my grandmother and my mother, and everything I had learned from them all rolled into the line." Beyoncé stated that she designs the clothing in House of Deréon in a forward-looking style. However, Beyoncé does not simply disregard the past. When asked who inspires her, Beyoncé named several people. However, Tina Knowles, her mother, is high on the list. One of the inspirations for the clothing, like the related jewelry, is Beyoncé's close relationship with her mother. However, she has a bigger vision for her customers. Business is not about big profits, Beyoncé claims in the interview. It's about teaching girls that "class and elegance are timeless."

BeyGOOD Foundation

On the webpage of the BeyGOOD Foundation, the mission statement is as follows: "BeyGOOD is a global charity and social impact initiative co-founded by Beyoncé in 2013. BeyGOOD exists to change the world, one act of kindness at a time. It operates with the heart of making a positive impact in our world through programming that takes action around our biggest challenges."

Causes At the time of writing this report, there are 10 different causes the foundation operates in. This includes helping to end hunger, making water available to every human being, reducing poverty, advancing education, providing housing and helping with rent, expanding mental health support, aiding in disaster response, improving general health issues and access to health care education, women in sport, and boosting women's economic power. Initiatives vary significantly across the 10 causes. The foundation has run a prize draw for a large festival in 2014, a national public awareness day for health policy in 2015, and a summer camp for children who survived Katrina in 2016. BeyGOOD teamed up with the First Lady of Alabama in 2015 and gave out free tickets to the award show in the mainland of the state. A social media campaign was launched to promote the First Lady's actions towards obesity prevention. In 2020, Beyoncé's foundation teamed up with the NAACP, a civil rights organization, to provide grants for black-owned small businesses in Houston, Texas. In 2021, BeyGOOD supported children affected by Hurricane Ida by distributing gift cards and hygiene kits and has also provided grants to organizations that work in the field of mental health, loss, and grief, as well as those who operate in the field of career and education.

8

Chapter 6: Beyoncé's Influence on Pop Culture

One of the most intriguing elements of Beyoncé's iconic status is the heavy influence she has assumed in relation to pop culture and the entertainment industries at large. Her influence intersects with many different fields, from music to film, fashion, popular culture, and even contemporary art. The following chapter will investigate how Beyoncé has been able to use her popularity to shape pop culture and solidify her status as a cultural icon, as well as her role in contemporary feminism and discourse.

Beyoncé and Her Status as a Cultural Icon

Beyoncé has long been an iconic figure in popular culture – commercials, movies, and fashion trends are all affected by the Beyoncé aesthetic. Perhaps of even greater significance is her critique of the record industry and its competition, her role in remixing genres, and her near-constant presence in the entertainment media. This chapter investigates the ways in which Beyoncé has shaped pop culture, particularly through her status as a resilient cultural icon and performer.

Beyoncé has a significant influence on popular music culture. A look back at national and international performances in 2016 will testify to her pervasive cultural footprint. In fact, so many paradigms have been influenced or altered by the Beyoncé phenomenon that it bears mention how aspects of performance, music industry consumerism and records, celebrity, and musical performance aesthetics, as well as common sense and entertainment narratives, have all been impacted.

Super Bowl Halftime Show Performances

Beyoncé has given three of the most memorable halftime performances at the Super Bowl football championship. These appearances in 2013, 2016, and 2019 represent core performances that reveal how the artist exemplifies a technological and commercial conception of rhythmic expression, how she uses rhythmic expression to craft politically dramatic presentations of gender and racial identity, and how she invites a response that recognizes those performances as exemplary.

In those performances, Beyoncé reconfirmed the cultural and commercial capital that her brand has accumulated over three decades. She invited these spectators to see the influence of black costuming, gestures, and "swag teeming with blackness," not in the ways in which it has rarely changed, but as part of the scene she was creating at that moment within the game broadcast's mise-en-scène. Beyoncé makes a break between a sleight of history that consigns herself, black women, and Destiny's Child to the bin of the "superfluous" and a gesture of Afro-fortune that pinpoints how she can overcome this relegation by living flamboyantly in front of an unseeing white gaze. Beyoncé's mere mention of the number at that mic in the moment that it was mentioned was a return of the repressed black performance, a raised fist pointing right at the excluded medio-melody rattling in each of those audible excesses. The performance that ensued from there offered to build an entire musical universe around that habit of extraction Beyoncé's name performed on. Begin your thinking about Beyoncé in the places where the name has brought you toward blackface distractibility and yield your task attentively to consider those sites' presentation of injustice.

Viral Moments

The greatest achievement of a superstar is making the transition from celebrity to phenomenon. There are few living people on earth who have accomplished this. Secretly and loudly, the whole world listens for what Beyoncé is going to do next month, and she never disappoints. She is queen; she is goddess; she walks on water and water parts because she walks on it. Wherever Beyoncé goes, she leaves viral moments in her wake, moments animated by her extraordinary beauty, her prodigious talent, and her shut-the-front-door cultural significance, a trinity unique unto her. Here Beyoncé is nothing less than Columbus in her navy Balmain dress, and her hair gathers frenziedly at the sides of her head like a cyclone. Beyoncé doing anything—singing, strolling through traffic, perusing a Doritos snack bag at a professional basketball game—immediately becomes the dance at Cupid's wedding.

She transcends even the most gif-able of us—with apologies to Sailor Senshi, how else to explain Beyoncé essentially becoming the lead character of "Cosmos" when she dropped her surprise self-titled album at the end of last year? Her work alone is practically viral distribution bait, like The Bible in Meow Meow Beenz society. Yet perhaps it was inevitable given that the spirit of her music was democratizing in a way that few pop stars are. It's worth noting that an artist described as "reclusive" can still be a massive star because of the internet. It might not even happen at all.

9

Chapter 7: The Formation World Tour

The final chapter of the book is also the longest. It was originally published as a separate article in The Black Scholar (date). The sources include the materials from the European tour that immediately followed the American circulation. Section 1 reviews the components of the concert-videos presented during the event and some of the reviews released in the first three shows. The text analyzes several points of the show, including the shocking visuals at the impact of the opening scene, the political potency of the set list (and sites of performance) and how Beyoncé performs in interaction with her company and with the audience. Section 2 provides a quote from Beyoncé about her aspirations for the tour and a review of shows in Detroit and Houston. The chapter presents a close reading of Beyoncé's 2016 multi-disciplinary performance event that includes context on her career to date and the rise of the grand scale concert tour.

The seventh chapter of this book is a consideration of the 2016-2017 Formation World Tour, from its opening at Marlins Park in Miami, Florida on April 27, 2016 to its closing at the MetLife Stadium in East Rutherford, New Jersey on October 7, 2016. The 77 shows that comprised the tour drew over 2.2 million ticket buyers and grossed over \$256 million. The chapter considers the production, music, politics and artistry of the event while also charting the development of a writer who has engaged with Beyoncé's work since the days of Destiny's Child and the final night of the On The Run tour in Paris in 2014, when Beyoncé and her husband Jay-Z performed under the stars of Illumination of Joan of Arc: Tony-Oursler-After Delphie (2012).

10

Chapter 8: Beyoncé's Visual Albums

The last two offerings of Beyoncé's discography are "visual albums." This format strikes me as intriguing because it once again defies traditional methods of music release. The visual album is generally an 'album' in name only. For instance, Beyoncé from 2014 is fifteen tracks and thirty-two videos - one for each track with an additional three bonus videos. Each of the visuals was released on YouTube at the same time as the album itself, leading to visual albums having streams through example stopgap services like Tidal which integrate the audio-only songs and the videos for their metrics, leading to astronomical impression counts. The music video has had a long history as an aesthetically interesting aspect to an artist's visual expression. Where Beyoncé is concerned, her extras can sometimes be more telling or of interest than the rest of the video. Her visual albums are, for lack of a better word, movies. But what it is about them that makes them fundamentally films and not extended music videos is not just quantity.

Throughout her career, Beyoncé's ability as a storyteller, along with the work that goes into crafting her image for viewers to maintain her position as both the most important member of Destiny's

Child and as Queen Bey, have been contingent on her star image in relation to independent ideals. Once she broke out of the mold made for her by popular conceptions, it was also important for her to tell her story as she wishes it to be seen. Her visual albums are her direct line of communication with the public and the consumer. Because Bonus Tracks isn't the soundtrack to a movie, but the movie and the album are essentially inseparable from one another, I believe both faithful and critical readings of Beyoncé's oeuvre benefit from an analysis of said album. Her movies are her audiovisuals. And to hear them is to see them is to understand her.

Lemonade

The opening chapter of this volume offers an introduction to Beyoncé's sixth studio album Lemonade. This introduction provides an explanation of the album's cultural and personal significance, as well as the choice to focus on it as the centerpiece of its own section of the book. Lemonade is an hour-long visual album released alongside a "road map" book containing the lyrics to the songs, published by Beyoncé in 2016. Lemonade is known for its tracklist, which proceeds through different emotional states characteristic of the grieving process: Intuition, Denial, Anger, Apathy, Emptiness, Accountability, Reformation, Forgiveness, Hope, and Redemption. The book goes with the album, functioning as a libretto or score. It is a collection of poetry, a story about the ostracization of an unfaithful partner and the recovery of a woman from that loss including references to Yoruba deities and to Judeo-Christian mythology.

The chapter delves into the individual implications and meanings of key songs in its own section, offering analysis and examples of Beyoncé's work during different moments of the album. These scholars use feminist, contemporary African American culture, and African diasporic theoretical frameworks in Cultural Studies in their work, providing a selection of frame-interpretations of the album in its wider popular culture context. Significantly, the album unites narrative and visual art production with cleverly layered racial, sexual, and feminist-political interpretations. Beyoncé is one of the leading female visual artists of today, managing the semiotics of music videos, album artwork, and visual albums across a wide range of platforms. In this introductory chapter, this volume argues that Lemonade can and should also be read in light of contemporary and contemporary visual arts contexts and practices.

Black is King

Released on 31 July 2020 on streaming service Disney Plus, Beyoncé's Black is King has been described as a visual album that reimagines the tale told in Disney's 2019 blockbuster The Lion King for "today's young kings and queens of the diaspora." Black Is King has collaborated with several artists from African countries to create original music videos. The film is a "recasting of a beloved cultural touchstone" with some of "contemporary culture's most notable voices." The film makes a resolutely positive statement. Speaking to The Washington Post, Bruce Wigo, who worked as a producer on the 1994 Lion King and several Lion King sequels, called "with one voice" the filmmakers' decision to "avoid Africa's real problems" a good one. They used the occasion of the first-ever sequel to a Disney animated classic to show "our world as it should be," he said. "That," Wigo told The Washington Post, "in the end, is a good thing".

In "Black is King," the pop star makes it clear that "if you want to see real, authentic Africa, Africa as it should be," you have to look to the diaspora. Her film is a globe-trotting journey through the Black world, from New York to Los Angeles to South Africa to Nigeria. For Adia N. Dunn, Black is King represents a profound rupture in the fabric of reality as it unfolds. As it is performed and visualized by Beyoncé, our reigning queen of popular culture iconography, Black is King is imbued with the power to foretell what is to come. Made possible by her significant financial, technological, and artistic resources, the film offers to us, her audience, the chance to see the world she sees and in turn to see its expansive potential. To wander the Kingdom in all its majesty is to be compelled beyond mere imagination and into a realm in which Black vision has the power to materialize at will. "In many ways," Dunn writes, "Black is King is prophecy." To BIC's exploration to explore—alongside Beyoncé's visual narrative and her own cultural references—work produced by artists and scholars who have thought Sky and the ways in which it has been taken up by institutions. "Like the visual album, which deftly and stunningly collaborates with a litany of artists and opportunities," Seats writes, "our dossier reflects an array of conversations that extend from the known and familiar to the strange and new, from the persistent challenges we face as audiences of culture to the euphoric potential of experiencing black art, making black culture, and seeing black life."

11

Chapter 9: The Lion King and Disney Partnership

This chapter offers a comprehensive overview of how Disney cast her, Walt Disney Studios' live-action film The Lion King's music, which she has produced along with vocal talent. In-depth analysis and interpretations of Beyoncé's role, performance, input into the album, and performance of the "Spirit" single from The Lion King: The Gift album. The chapter explores Beyoncé's synergy and artistic collaborations with Disney, her and Jay-Z's shutting down Disneyland music video for "Apesh*t", Kanye's 'Disney-fied' joint Vogue shoot with Kim and North in August 2018, and The Lion King: The Gift's position in Disney's soundtrack production, marketing, and distribution strategies. It further explores The Lion King's cultural impact: the importance of the representation of modern 21st-century African-ness, the fantasy world produced by the film, and a critical look at the film's portrayal of lions.

Beyoncé describes with great confidence how her characteristic 'anger' energy and individual sentiments and intentions in regards to Lyricist Tim Rice's 'He Lives In You' shape the acting of Simba's character in Disney's The Lion King. A song that featured in the musical, 'He Lives In You' is an adaptation of Lebo M's African chant from the first animated film. Her brief and rich commentary bears striking similarities to how she engages with developing the albums for the original The Lion King and The Lion King: The Gift. Beyoncé describes working on the song for the original soundtrack as something simple and very Steve McQueen, which to her means sitting on a master's chair to record the vocals. Sho'nuff - McQueen's garage workshop is the setting of Master's (Julius Carry) last fight in The Last Dragon. The music Beyoncé produces with Disney for the following album is African-inspired.

12

Chapter 10: Black Lives Matter and Social Activism

Beyoncé's involvement in Black Lives Matter is not confined to her art, though it certainly includes it. Instead of asking pro Bernie Sanders questions, when she sings, "You might be up one day, then you turn around and lose it all," she stands emphatically for #BlackLivesMatter and gets people at the Super Bowl to follow her lead. She released a 560-word statement concerning police who intimidate, harass, threaten, and otherwise stop black lives from "looking like that." In Louisiana, this meant a helicopter, military gear, and devastating gunfire leaving six children post-police action suffering in households relegated to "very, very destroyed." Beyoncé and Joshua DuBois understand social justice as intimately connected to her commitment to forward progress. DuBois writes, "And as we were ending the call, the President kicked off the 21st century version of what used to be called a barnstorm, made famous by Harry Truman, getting out of Washington to talk to the American people, but in the new millennium, it involves newspaper editorials and websites, a private lunch with opinion writers and columnists, this one was on the record, and a radio interview with NPR's Steve Inskeep. And among the things that the President wanted to talk about was to make sure that people understood the inspiration that he drew from some of these folks who took the time to come to the Oval Office. And that's one of the things that he did in this forum as well."

Donations and Support

The Beyoncé Phenomenon: From Destiny's Child to Queen Bey - The Beyoncé Phenomenon: Essays on Sexuality, Race, and Feminism

Beyoncé's philanthropic support often seems to go hand in hand with the messages she conveys through her art. Doing good in the world is what is on her agenda in her personal life as well as in her music. She is aware of her privilege, as is illustrated by her claim: "I just think it's important to give support to a cause that can make the world a better place."

Regarding the various forms of support Beyoncé gives, the most visible might be the "I Was Here" video, in which she wore a Versace pantsuit as she slowly made her way through a backstage hallway to the stage where she appeared with a chorus of young people in black t-shirts who had been volunteering at the United Nations for their 67th General Assembly to commemorate World Humanitarian Day. The video of Beyoncé, shot in a hard-edged, almost frenetic style, is intercut with footage of humanitarian workers, some of them quite young, in dangerous and strenuous situations from sites including New York, the Philippines, Malawi, Haiti, Vietnam, Nepal, Sri Lanka, and Turkey. The chorus was diverse; the footage showed the kids singing, holding candles, painting, and tirelessly offering aid to people in need from around the world. Although she used the phrase "send it to death" after her performance and explained the project was "about helping people; but not donating, not watching the kids," "I Was Here" turned out to be her publicity vehicle.

Public Statements

The social role of Beyoncé has defined her as an advocate in her team of professionals to adapt to their historical and social context and public opinion that is built on the artistic work of the singer. Beyoncé has stopped being a popstar to become a public figure defending social justice in public protests across the United States. On July 9, 2016, Beyoncé issued a request to her millions of followers: #Freedom. Her show coincided with the same day that the violence exploded across the United States for police killings towards the public of African American humorist. It was the fourth night of protests in New York and Washington capital and Beyoncé took advantage of the scenario to make a loud and public statement. However, her search for controversy did not end here. Formed within the African American community, Beyoncé proclaimed her right to be black openly, claiming to be "proud of her heritage."

Beyoncé's social fighting power is more than one day and more than one word. In Jacksonville, Florida, in 2013, Beyoncé asked for a moment of silence at Dora's rehearsals, a moment enshrined to honor the memory of Jordan Davis, the football player who died in July 2012. Now she wants to directly face the public. In Toronto, at the Mrs. Manning concert, she chose a quote to serve as a statement that would precede her the boys every time it was sung. "All lives can be blessed until black lives are important," he said. In Beyoncé's Sacramento concert, a "Flash Luminoso Human" movement was created with powerful phrases of protest "black life matters". Does anyone who has lost relatives, has experienced marginalization, or has been a victim of racial discrimination in the United States come to an annual cookie in the spring? "I want to know," she said.

In September 2016, Beyoncé was about 50% full, and reverend be-gan to lecture during her concert. In 1981, Beyoncé and her family were part of the largest tour group in North America. Just as her mother instilled the hope and optimism of the day, Beyoncé sees the present and the future from her personal point of view. A year of transportation, odyssey and struggle ended in the United States. I wondered why now.

13

Chapter 11: The Carters:
Beyoncé and Jay-Z

Reports of the first relationship between Jay-Z and Beyoncé surfaced in 2002—the same year they would "work together on the single '03 Bonnie & Clyde'." Then, in interviews about the track, the performers maintained that they were just "friends." Rumors about their possible offstage romantic involvement continued to circulate even after the respective ends of Jay-Z's association with his girlfriend of some two years, singer Amil, and Beyoncé's long-term boyfriend, TV actor Mos Def. In fact, after working together for the first time on "'03 Bonnie & Clyde," they spent the year 2003 performing with Missy Elliott on the "TRL" tour, collaborating on hit records, and buying matching luxury cars. Both took offense at the suggestion that they might be dating. "Beyoncé's so much more talented than you could ever imagine," Jay-Z told a representative of the St. Louis Post-Dispatch in 2003. "She can sing, dance, and move." He added, "She's beautiful" as an afterthought. Meanwhile, while denying that anything was going on between herself and Jay-Z, Beyoncé described him to Diane Sawyer as an "incredible," "honest" "visionary" who was "every woman's fantasy" but was also, she added, "different for every woman." "But no..." she concluded, "we're not together." However, it was in the year 2003 that the partnership between Jay-Z and Beyoncé as business associates also began to take shape. Open disagreement about the nature of their relationship ceased after the release of the scandalous "Crazy In Love." A collaboration between Jay-Z, Beyoncé, producer Rich Harrison, and rapper Sean Paul of the Jamaica-based group the Dutty Rock-crew, "Crazy In Love" was the talk of 2003. Surgeon General Richard Carmona called the single "never-endingly infectious." It garnered Grammy nominations, MTV Music Video awards and Viewer Choice Awards. After a five-week blitz, the record went double platinum and spent twenty-plus weeks in the Billboard Top 100. A concrete release of the same name was a recruitment tool for the U.S. Army. Aggressive encomiums for Beyoncé's physique led to interracial comparisons involving black and white female media personalities. Chris Rock suggested that an "ugly white girl" would not still be a big star after dancing provocatively next to herself in a video. Carson Daly suggested that Beyoncé was one of the "great women of all time." "There's not a lot of chicks I fantasize about," he said, "but that white tank top, forget about it." Beyoncé, "standing near the end of the world behind two vintage Cadillac convertibles that looked as if they'd been custom-designed to please Barbie and her friends," licked "a-one-two-three o'clock-four". Berry's "slinky girl's outfit" came off with its "strip-club sparkle" to reveal a cream-colored "slinky girl's bathing suit". "There are other ways a woman could be holding herself in this crisis," the writer hypothesizes, "but we know what this kind of girl is going to do." Beyoncé's "single-minded subjectivity" was illustrated to readers through analysis of the behavior of three former Destiny's Child stylists.

Relationship Beginnings

In 2000, Beyoncé was the lead singer of Destiny's Child, and Jay-Z was a rising rapper who was also the co-founder and chief executive of the newly incensed recording company Roc-A-Fella Records. Armed with the support of their respective professional teams of public relations advisors, stylists, and Boston-based, reluctant-to-make-the-cross-country trip hairdresser, Beyoncé and Jay-Z collaborated in the recording studio for the first time. Contrary to popular rumors, they did not arrive together for that recording session or embark hand-in-hand on a journey of love as predestined soul mates. In fact, no sexual tension nor particularly compelling magnetism gripped them upon their initial person-to-person contact. Rather, M+R Platinum's (Beyoncé's management team) efforts to arrange a meeting between Jay-Z and Beyoncé consisted of two failed attempts before they finally met in the recording studio that sunny day four years ago.

While Jay admired Beyoncé, and both clearly were at least physically attracted to each other, the idea of collaborating on a song simply occurred. This professional, musical union led to infrequent and casual encounters often described in the popular press as "big brother/little sister" meetings over the years. All the while, the pair demonstrated a nonchalance about what tabloids speculated regarding the nature of their relationship. The extent of their romance over the years had largely been confined to brief and sporadic exchanges between takes in the recording studio, the duration of which, generally, fell closely in line with Jay-Z's meetings at the record label offices. In the public eye, Jay-Z maintained a long-term relationship with a Caribbean woman he was engaged to, and Beyoncé was involved in infrequent flings, the genuineness of her reported relationships very much open to question.

Collaborations

All three names are featured in this chapter as the destinies of Shawn Carter, Beyoncé, and Jay-Z are now more intertwined than ever. The chapter starts with a narrative of the twenty-year-old Beyoncé stepping onto the set of "'03 Bonnie and Clyde" and meeting the man who would reappear in her life and art twelve years later as "the one." In the collaborative year of 2003, Beyoncé and Jay-Z's high-profile relationship crossed over into music in the form of that first duet, on Jay's The Black Album. By 2008, Beyoncé and Jay-Z were declaring common kingship through a wedding band and a tandem tour. Throughout most of these years, Jay-Z was the world's foremost rapper and Beyoncé was his popular little wife. However, in 2011, Beyoncé famously ran the world. That year, she was everywhere, singing an epoch-defining single with unexpected political resonances. The suffix "-mance" often refers to lovers.

Musical and cinematic collaborations resulted in the coupling of business interests. Since then, her career and album Lemonade became the subject of worldwide speculation. Suddenly, we could not stop talking about Beyoncé and Jay-Z. Jay-Z became a personal subject of a song entitled Lemonade that Beyoncé performed on the biggest world stage: the Super Bowl. According to BMI filings, Jay-Z was officially being credited as a licensee of Beyoncé's music as early as her 2005 solo debut, and the two later contended that they were music publishers of a body of work that included everything from "Crazy in Love" to the critically acclaimed Lemonade. However, the most formally mutual work the two musicians jointly published was Everything Is Love, released in collaboration with the Cartername-formed Roc Nation label in June 2018. The album's release was an extravagant surprise to fans: the promotion for it included a music video filmed in the Louvre, the first time the museum opened its doors to a commercial music video. In 2019, the album won the prize for Best Urban Contemporary Album at the 19th Grammy Awards, where it was nominated in three categories. The song "Apeshit" was nominated in the categories for Best Music Video and Best Rhythm and Blues Song. The album had several songs appear on music charts across the globe, the song "Apeshit" even being nominated for record of the year at the Grammy's in 2019. Everything Is Love also corroborates the idea that Beyoncé and Jay-Z belong to the category of blockbuster musicians. Nearly fifteen years into their careers as artists, Beyoncé and Jay-Z continue to draw the attention of critics, scholars, and casual fans of popular music. Their long orbits of superstardom, marked by the union of their family in 2008, left the public always on the lookout for new intratextual revelations.

14

Chapter 12: Beyoncé's Film Roles

In the film One True Thing (1998), the protagonist, Ellen Gulden, played by Meryl Streep, complains to her husband: "I get away from my daughter the only time in six years for three hours. I change into clothes that are too tight, expose collagen-injected lips, and listen to lyrics that aren't music." The lyrics she heard were coming from Destiny's Child on stage singing "Bills, Bills, Bills." Reflecting the connections between music and film, the two worlds blur where superstar idols from one have parallel careers in the other. Ellen Gulden was actually listening to Kelly Rowland, LeToya Luckett, LaTavia Roberson, and, of course, Beyoncé Knowles sing one of their most popular tunes produced by Kevin "She'kspere" Briggs, member of the production team The Cavaliers. While many recording artists try to "act," and there are certainly many examples of both musicians who have succeeded in film and some who have failed, the proximity between Cyrus's and Beyoncé's is striking.

The Beyoncé phenomenon goes beyond film alone. For example, some of her music is used on the movie's soundtrack which is also contributing to her multidimensional artistic talents and abilities. This essay has discussed Beyoncé's film appearances in a variety of contexts and genres. It is not an exhaustive examination of her screen outings as an actress, nor does it present detailed stylistic and formal analysis of the films or the narrative and characterization devices used by Beyoncé. Rather, this chapter focuses on the role of music and the intersection of acting as a singer. In particular, the essay argues that more critical attention should be paid to Beyoncé's contributions to screen culture and the implications of her celebrity impact within the acting world.

Dreamgirls

To celebrate the premiere of Tom Hooper's screen adaptation of Cats that was released in late 2019, Vulture, the New York Magazine website, published an article speculating which 21st-century superstar would fill each role in Webber's musical. Unsurprisingly, the article suggested that Beyoncé would join the A-list cast. This is a standard Hollywood narrative: the singer who rules the popular realm now transforms into an actress. Beyoncé has acted before, of course, but How to Make Lemonade claims that the project—a big-budget, wider-released shoulder into film-stardom conducted under a white, male director—was different and more complicated: "As the lead role in a traditional film musical, all dressed in vintage face powder, Beyoncé glammed up for a part both safe and emblematic. While critics loved her performance in Dreamgirls (just she hope she gets an Oscar!), the untroubling image of the queen diva's first (and possibly last) day in old Hollywood was cannier, drawing on and adding to her most successful public identity "Beyoncé" (218). This chapter complicates the Dreamgirls angle, testing How to Make Lemonade argument that the Dreamgirls role was a merely replicative, unworthy performance.

Yet Dreamgirls, with Beyoncé in a leading role, is too pivotal to leave out of the popular-public version of her career. Dreamgirls the captivating and failed reconciliation of Beyoncé's pop fame with the film-musical genre of past times. Some critic celebrate this union, as the New York Times called, "Beyoncé's phenomenal, fourth-gear breakthrough performance in Dreamgirls." These celebrations make Beyoncé and the movie easier to consume as art: they are just so good. And for those who have heard the news (or read the entire chapter), Dreamgirls is a turning point in Beyoncé's evolution as "Queen Beyoncé," the mononymous diva.

The Lion King

Mrs. Carter has always kept her eye on long-lasting Hollywood royalty, but she managed to do so without parting with her divinely self-professed humility - until The Lion King, that is. The Disney revival reaped the benefits of an extended premiere weekend; more importantly, it gifted audiences with a Beyoncé big enough to match Beychella. Parkwood Entertainment and Walt Disney Records released an accompanying album, The Lion King: The Gift, on July 19, a few hours before box-office talliers tweeted that audiences were already retracing the steps of their childhood to catch another glimpse of Simba and Mufasa.

The pack of eleven tracks feature two Beyoncé leads, "Bigger" (a grittier "Spirit" moment) and the Burna Boy-assisted "Ja Ara e," as well as notable contribution from Blue Ivy on the remarkably well-performed "Brown Skin Girl." Die-hards admired Queen Bey's stretch into Afrobeat territory on Twitter, hailing her for yet another relentless - and shrewd - rebrand. Film critics spent the week after the premiere parsing the details of Beyoncé's acclaimed, Disney-funded pursuit as inspiring orchid to the otherwise computer-animated, choirlike visuals that dictate the film's newborn image. On Wednesday, Beyoncé unveiled a documentary about the making of the record. Social media exploded over the weekend to a mode of passive admiration, acknowledging that, like everything else in the multifac-eted Beyoncé industry of things, The Lion King had come out, and it had made its mark.

15

Chapter 13: Awards and Achievements

It was clear even after Destiny's Child won their first Grammy in 2001 that Beyoncé was special. But could the world have known that, in the more than 20 years since, she would become the most awarded female artist? How magnificent and idiosyncratic is she? Would any other do, eh? In this chapter, come with us to retrace the meteoric heights of her reign.

Awards and Achievements The numbers don't lie: 24 wins at the Billboard Music Awards; 28 at the MTV Video Music Awards; 7 at the American Music Awards; 8 at the BET Awards; 28 at the Billboard Women in Music Awards; and a whopping 85 nominations and twelve wins at the Grammy Awards—a decade's worth of wins, racking in over 80 nominations total. In 2020, she broke the record for the most wins at the BET Awards, with an awe-inspiring 31 in total. Her Simple of the Year forehead isn't too shabby either: ranked in the top 25 on Forbes' Celebrity 100 list for ten years, including seven top 10 finishes. Speaking of Forbes, in 2014, she snatched the number one spot on the publication's annual Celebrity 100 list, boasting estimated annual earnings to the tune of $115 million.

And it isn't solely about numbers, right? On 5 January 2020, she became the first black woman to win the award for Best Original Song at the Golden Globes. She won the award for "Spirit," her contribution to the 2019 Lion King reboot, which is a fantastic example of the monthly money moves I otherwise probably would not have been aware of. In 2016, she made history at the Emmy Awards after "Lemonade" was slapped with four nods, including Outstanding Variety Special. Her brand of Midas Touch has resulted in four special honors to recognize this remarkable achievement: the Millennium of Honour at the 2000 World Music Awards and the Billboard Millennium Award at the 2011 Billboard Music Awards. In 2016, she was also honored with the Michael Jackson Video Vanguard Award at the MTV Video Music Awards.

16

Chapter 14: Criticism and Controversies

Despite rave reviews and her overwhelmingly strong fan base, Beyoncé Knowles has not been without her fair share of criticism and controversy for the spate of diverse activities and comments. Some cultural critics evaluate Beyoncé's various appearances with a lack of discernment, while others question her role as a performer who constructs and enforces the standards of normativity, respectability, and proximity as if such stances are driven purely by her material gain. It is proposed that these evaluations have simplistic subtexts because they do not take into consideration the opportunities that enable Knowles to encounter considerable success in the popular music industry. Furthermore, these contrarian criticisms do not take into consideration the complexities of female desire, sexual display, and self-management, as depicted in both Beyoncé's lyrics and images as well as in a plurality of other pop performers.

Those purposes, shaped by personal biography and business practice, are inextricably intertwined with respectability insofar as the strictures and rewards of appearing—and occasionally desiring—to appear normative have inextricable consequences in Beyoncé Inc. Some corporate controversies have led to the potential of her reputation being tarnished, including failed absolved endorsement deals, duos and engagements with masculine luxury goods and automobiles, and a number of charitable concerts by her and, later, her newest amour. Although closely controlled, her career saturates the Internet and other mass media and maintains a high cultural momentum, regardless of whether she is resting between album releases or actively promoting a new project. The experiences and expectations of diverse fan populations cannot be reduced or decided by the various evaluations of so-called critics. In order to summarize the various readings to which Beyoncé has been subjected and to distill the significance of all those readings, I have addressed a plethora of possible critiques in this book, before offering up a guide for the production and consumption of Beyoncé.

Lip-Syncing Controversy

In January 2013, three years after her electrifying live inauguration performance of "At Last" for the Obamas, Beyoncé faced a lip-syncing controversy in the news media. In a proposed article on the "public examination of spectacle," Grasso argued that Beyoncé inspires such rigorous debate because of her divisive persona, products, and performances. Grasso contends that she is powerful, popular, and prosperous because of a fundamental, logical, political, and profitable formula: Beyoncé + spectacle = scrutiny = money and power.

Beyoncé faced lip-syncing accusations, vitriol, and mockery after her barnstorming live performance of "The Star-Spangled Banner" during President Barack Obama's second inauguration on January 21, 2013. She had pre-recorded it the Sunday before with the backing of the United States Marine Band in the case of inclement weather. Beyoncé managed to silence her detractors with her Mercury-mimicking Super Bowl halftime show, ear and eyeball-shattering guest appearances on London radio and national talk shows, and on February 3 through her face-off against her female stakeholders in the so-called "HarBowl" at Super Bowl XLVII (47). This manipulation of live reality and media representation outraged some, but Beyoncé's talent rallies make even her begrudgers reconciliationists.

The inaugural lip-syncing controversy and news media firestorm underscored some fundamental challenges Beyoncé faced in her role as a female recording artist. This surprisingly entertaining, unexpected opportunity to entertain occurred in the celebrity-friendly milieu of television news with more than 38 million viewers during Anderson Cooper 360°, Sean Hannity's Hyped Culture, Piers Morgan Tonight, and the rhetorical reclaimed feminist Rachel Maddow Show. Megan Garber (2013) described Beyoncé as "a soldier of capitalism," one who "was the key item on offer in America, Inc." on that "big day of civic America, Inc." in January 2013. Beyoncé's performances will always raise suspicion because these two symbolic facets dictate two intolerant rules: no one can possibly "look that good" legions of betrayers argue, and she might appear to lip-sync because she dances too much for any normal human being to be able to belt out such lyrics in real time.

Cultural Appropriation Debate

Critics across the board have scrutinized Beyoncé's use of largely African American stereotypes and discourses. They see her as a beneficiary of her privileged position in the mainstream pop industry to the detriment of other less fortunate - and darker skinned - African American women. According to the analysis advanced by Olden, by sporting golden jewelry, bleached wavy hair, and somewhat lighter makeup, Beyoncé adopts a more mainstream look that distinguishes her from other black women. Olden uses feminist psychoanalytic theories to argue that Beyoncé uses bright paint and sparkles to mask the impurities of blackness and femininity evidenced by the lyrics of her song "Partition" (2013). She thus uncannily masks her despised "n*****'ness" to conform more closely to white, male standards of beauty.

She has been co-opting mainstream discourses about women, motherhood, and sexuality to create spectacular images that operate as convoluted commentaries on contemporary race relations, sexual politics, and representational issues. By drawing on the varied interpretations circulated in numerous "think" pieces, The Beyoncé Phenomenon seeks to grasp the richness of criticisms, analyses, responses, blogging, retweets, reposts, rants, and Instagram comments about Beyoncé's musical, cultural, political, and personal significance. However, while I appreciate these varied interpretations and often agree with much of the critique of her repressed and vibrant shady speculative aspects, I aim to provide a more complex analysis of Beyoncé's repertoires of spectacular femininity using theories of psychoanalysis and critical race theory.

17

Chapter 15: Beyoncé's Fashion Evolution

In this chapter, I explore the ways in which Beyoncé's fashion aesthetic has evolved, look at some of her most influential fashion moments, and examine the different moments at which Beyoncé has effectively utilized fashion in the representation of her artistic persona. This analysis presents Beyoncé as a fashion icon who has developed the capacity to both reflect and shape the cultures in which she is a key participant. In the building of Beyoncé's music career over the course of more than two decades, the significance of her clothing choices has frequently been documented. The Fashion Spot, for instance, keeps a blog of every outfit Beyoncé is seen wearing with a view to tracking her impact on the international fashion landscape.

This is also due to the fact that Beyoncé has always been particularly fashion-conscious. The singer reflects on how she has always been more interested in the clothing and styling of performances than in the music before her. In a Rock and Roll Hall of Fame Q&A session in the early 2000s, Beyoncé stated: "I was in Destiny's Child and Nick at Nite would show these old shows, and I saw Diana Ross and the Supremes. I was surrounded by all these fabulous, glamorous girls and sequined dresses," and added, "I loved the music, but

I really loved the dresses." From the beginning of her career, therefore, Beyoncé has been deeply interested in the representation of herself as persona-in-concert, and in particular, how fashion impacts this. Fashion's heavy presence in much of the footage that surrounds Beyoncé's public persona contributes a vital layer of understanding to the meanings she is seen to generate. This fashion interest has defined the segments of the entertainment industry in which she has successfully operated.

18

Chapter 16: Beyoncé's Philanthropic Work

The previous chapters have presented an exploration of Beyoncé's philanthropy, from initial projects in her early career right through to her hallmark initiatives. This chapter aims to outline a detailed explanation of Beyoncé's charitable work, both by utilizing online content and key informant interviews. This chapter explicates not only Beyoncé's charitable work, but the responses to her philanthropy and the direct impact of her donations and partnerships.

This chapter provides an in-depth and comprehensive breakdown of Beyoncé's philanthropic work throughout her career, presenting it in chronological order. The chapter also examines critical and popular responses to her philanthropy and the immediate impacts of her donations. This research highlights Beyoncé's publicized philanthropy and the impact of her donations. Beyoncé has redefined some of the public expectations around celebrities' social and moral obligations and challenged the supposed cynicism of the public toward this phenomenon. To this end, her philanthropy is shaped by social issues and her activism that goes beyond merely reactionary programs and media representations of transgressive bodies. This research has studied and celebrated Beyoncé's gifts and partnerships that go beyond her aesthetic appeal and contribute to communities that have, through her contributions to sociopolitical emancipation, only received broad media coverage. This end, while some of her critics and admirers find it troublesome and question the efficacy of her philanthropy, has sought to have a scholarly examination of the concrete impacts and value of her charitable practices.

Hurricane Relief Efforts

On September 4, 2005, just days after Hurricane Katrina made landfall in Louisiana, Beyoncé, Kelly Rowland, and Michelle Williams aired their "Destiny's Child: A Concert for Hurricane Relief" to support the United States victims of the disaster. On September 9, 2008, Beyoncé took a wider view with her participation in "Stand Up to Cancer" aimed at raising funds for "groundbreaking" cancer research. On September 12, 2009, she was starring in "Teleton México," a television program designed to raise money for the rehabilitation of children suffering from physical disabilities. Much more recently, she performed at her own 2017 "Hand in Hand" telethon that raised tens of millions of dollars in support of the U.S. communities affected by hurricanes and flooding. A close, but incomplete, transcription of their declared offers and remarks serves as evidence of these things. It describes their humanitarian activism while Beyoncé, Kelly, or Michelle perform on screen. It also provides raw data from which to learn more about how acts of philanthropy intersect with other forms of personal and political identity. Beyoncé's humanitarianism is not necessarily about Beyoncé at all times; it is also about the hurricane survivors. Her shows are reminders that survivors should not be forgotten. They are inspirational to listeners. They are badges of honor for the current climate of altruism in a pop entertainment industry where "philanthrocapitalism" is the "it" thing to do.

Scholarship Programs

In addition to creating music, Beyoncé has also contributed to the world of education. In 2017, she established the Formation Scholars Program, an academic scholarship designed to honor young women who are "bold, creative, conscious, and confident." One of the goals of the program is to show female students that their presence alone matters greatly. Since then, Beyoncé has continued supporting education through scholarship programs.

In April 2018, Beyoncé launched the Homecoming Scholars Award Program. The goal of these scholarships is to annually expand Beyoncé's global scholarship program and celebrate the 1-year anniversary of LEMONADE. According to Beyoncé, "We honor all institutions of higher learning for maintaining culture and creating environments for optimal learning." The aim is to offer students who are unafraid of new territory and have a light that is contagious – students who dream boldly and out loud. Furthermore, the scholarship programs emphasize that education is an investment for those who are serious about it and will use their education for greater good. Beyoncé is no stranger to sacrifice and hard work to achieve her dreams. More importantly, she is still dedicated to empowering young people seeking higher education either working towards a degree or certification program with funds to make college possible. Beyoncé's scholarships share in the mission of education. Beyoncé is not only changing the game in music and entertainment; she is also changing the game in educational opportunities for others. As of this research, she is giving away 50 scholarships worth $25,000.00 through 11 historically black colleges and universities. To date, she has supported over a thousand students through scholarship programs. While still climbing the billboards, Beyoncé's path to education is already a hit!

19

Chapter 17: The Impact of Beyoncé's Motherhood

Most of the attention given to Beyoncé and motherhood has centered on her transition into that role. Some criticism has been sparked by the relatively short time between the birth of her first and second child; there are those who comment on her daughter Ivy Blue in terms of her ethnicity and the length of her hair. Others criticize the way the Golden Throne Room photo of her pregnancy was digitally enhanced. In parallel, several feature articles have appeared in the press which praise her extraordinary performances, lists of her most accomplished songs and lyrics, or state that the singer has become a symbol of empowerment. They also argue that Beyoncé's transformation into a mother is expressed through her varied artistic output (music, videos, concerts, films, modeling, fashion designs) that have appeared since Blue Ivy Carter was born.

Beyoncé, it is said in various articles and interviews, has changed 'profoundly' since she became a mother. The strongest representation of her new persona is her single "Flawless," featuring feminist author Chimamanda Ngozi Adichie. In her most recent albums, which were accompanied by videos and world tours, the singer-songwriter revealed an unexpected side: a feminist vision expressed in often violent, aggressive lyrics, and in immodest appearances in public. Two parallel sides of her life and attitude towards her daughter came into being through her interviews and appearances. Beyoncé as a mother declared that the way she interacts with her daughter has changed her all-consuming love and interest in the child. Cultural commentators' positioning the singer in the cultural spectrum has been explored in single documentary films and discussions.

Blue Ivy

"Blue Ivy" is one of the fruits of this re-envisioned structure. This chapter offers a focused investigation of the significance of Beyoncé's eldest daughter. Her unique and highly discussed situation offers great insight into what it means to be the daughter of the most famous celebrity in the world. Special attention is paid to the public discourse, how Blue Ivy is portrayed in it and interpreted by it, as well as cultured. The interpretation that I seek to provide in this chapter is that Beyoncé's family-size image and sound reveal the powerful and illuminating language of myth as an inseparable part of how she moves across media. This is partly singular to Beyoncé as a highly unique celebrity figure, but it can also be seen as a broader and more general characteristic of this current media moment. As a consequence of seeing and valuing Beyoncé as a mythic figure, this chapter identifies the process of change and transformation that is initiated by her presence and/or disappearance from public life on a larger and broader scale.

"Blue Ivy" starts with a fresh news story. This narrative is designed to keep three versions of the same event from 2012 in play: the one reported in the gossip magazine Us Weekly, a different one reported in the following week's National Enquirer, and a very different one reported, also in January 2012, in the Brooklyn-run celebrity tabloid Star. Instead of setting these stories in chronological order, the introduction reads them chronologically. In so doing, I intensify their differences rather than smooth over them. After introducing these narratives, the chapter shifts gears and travels deep into the extensive media coverage of Blue Ivy's birth that appeared in mainstream news media in the United States and the extensive African and global blogosphere over the course of the next twenty-four hours. Along the way, it traces the press conference and image-as-ectoplasm that Beyoncé had appeared at the 1 OAK (One of a Kind) nightclub in New York five days after center of the central to the process of reading and interpreting these media discourses. This central feature is what a myth is when it occurs today, here, at the beginning of the twenty-first century, in and through the presence of Beyoncé, mothering and her husband fathering the most famous baby girl in today's world.

Twins Rumi and Sir

This stage in Beyoncé's life, like any woman, she has been a mother of twins. In what we know of her, and it's not a lot, she paints herself the image of a fulfilled, divinely graced mother of her new progeny. That Beyoncé is much in control of the experience of being a mum to her youngest children is without doubt. Their story will be her story and embodies an image that transcends the truth of their reality. Their presence in her life functions to bracket off that part: the early morning drudgery, the working out of other people's needs, the feelings of inadequacy, the private victories.

For Beyoncé, twin pregnancy becomes a feature of her life, part of her legend. It is, during its unfolding and into the future of history, an aspect of what we remember of her. She releases on Instagram into global consciousness an ethereal image of her heavily pregnant body clad in diaphanous veils flowing in the struggle of a new life force unfolding. It is a hark back to other eras, a cry to spirituality, the symbolic flowering of the mother of life on earth, a divine association, indeed Madonna's lament (Beyoncé as divine mother, or rather the mother of divinities, a tale of birth under the auspices of the gods as her public image, is here celebrated). Her twins are the first people she offers to the visual public to consume as private and free-floating fantasy, open for readers' dreams and projections.

20

Chapter 18: Beyoncé's Artistic Collaborations

Beyoncé's artistic partnerships, performances, entrepreneurial ventures, and creative alliances: indeed, Beyoncé has crafted many groundbreaking collaborations in music, business, and fashion. In terms of music and sound, she has engaged in remarkable collaborations that have defined the sonic direction of her work. However, she has also been involved in less remarked but highly influential collaborations where, through live performances, concerts, exhibitions, videos, and other outlets for showing visual images, she and her collaborators have had a striking impact on fashion, film, and indeed, on visual culture more generally. Furthermore, some of the best work produced through these collaborations is met with interpretive marginalization in the mainstream media. For years, Beyoncé's visual concept albums like B'Day (2006) and Lemonade (2016) have been accompanied by companion art exhibitions, bridging a very adult slipstream between stylized music video and high modernist visual art. Furthermore, over the years, observers of Beyoncé Knowles Carter (and there are masses of us) have been asked to 'taste' a little bit of the visual fashion high-life, looking through Lemonade-branded 'mash-up' clothing art/museums as well as videos that are strange amalgamations of some of Beyoncé's most awe-inspiring and controversial fashion statements. Beyoncé's contribution to film studies gets less influential attention than it deserves. With Lady Gaga and Estravenimity, she has collaborated with some of the most stylish and flashy filmmakers of our time. As Lady Gaga remarks, Beyoncé brings another level of sophistication and glamour to their collaborations, and she canonized some great directors in the process. Furthermore, one of the most ordinary places for major fashion launches and dreams/hopes for renewal resides in music videos. And, of course, Beyoncé has been very effective at changing established, archetypal modes of visuality via her music videos. 'Single Ladies' (2008) and 'Formation' (2016) are two standout examples of how Beyoncé has underscored dramatic changes in fashion via music videos, though there are many other examples as well. Each new musical direction that she makes producers, directors, and other collaborators work in conversation with her Bonde-inspired fashion as well as her music. This then gets circulated back into fashion and popular texts. As might be crystal clear by now, many of the most important visual texts in the 'speech' community of fashion refer to Beyoncé and exhibit complex character archetypes that appear to be inspired by her songs and visuals. In each case, Beyoncé moves mountains and changes the structures of visuality, often while pushing against the genre into this or that artistic.

Music Collaborations

In this selection of articles, we concentrate specifically on some of Beyoncé's significant musical partnerships. While different chapters may mention some of the well-known narratives of her life and career, we position these groups of writers as offering insights not only into the impact of her collaborative ventures, but also into the dynamics of these creative alliances, and the diversity of Beyoncé's musical connections. The authors in Chapters 19 and 21 look respectively at Beyoncé's collaborations with her father Mathew, and her sister Solange. L. Janelle Dance presents the argument that while Mathew was a central figure in Destiny's Child, post-From From to Bow, chapter 2016, Beyoncé has sought musical freedom from him and, at times, sought to distance herself from his management of her career.

Moving from the family unit to the Beyoncé/Jay-Z collaboration lends opportunities to discuss their personal, musical and, in particular, their vocal collaboration and how their 'American' image has been constructed. Jennifer D. Ryan analyses how, to promote their music, both Beyoncé and Jay-Z utilize their personal life. The final chapter in the Music section (Chapter 23) returns to focus specifically on the theme of childhood. Crystal Anderson and Chinita Lee Jones note that Beyoncé often claims that she was a child of the eighties, yet scholarship on eighties music hardly ever mentions her. In this article the authors set out to redress the critical imbalance by identifying three childhood musical figures that they argue influenced her, and through them provide an important, and often overlooked, basis for the future of the Queen Bey (the author's coinage), and the years of chart-topping and cultural dominance that have come to define her.

Fashion Collaborations

Beyoncé's many collaborations with fashion designers and brands show her relevance to the industry and appeal to widespread audiences. Prabal Gurung's line of T-shirts features a quote from Chimamanda Ngozi Adichie's "We Should All Be Feminists," which Beyoncé sampled in her song "Flawless" (2013): "Femininity is a mixture of both 'messy and magic,'" the T-shirts declare. We can read the quotation in combination with branding engagements to see how Beyoncé becomes part of fashion's ideology and ethics, and connects with the audience on the basis of her distinct modes of representation. As previous chapters have shown, Beyoncé has made many contributions to fashion and operates at an intersection of music celebrity and fashion celebrity. Among her many fashion collaborations, one can include her work to expand fashion into a lifestyle brand, to influence how fashion retail spaces decide to provide experience and storytelling on behalf of corporations, and how beauty, brands, and fashion can combine to give back to social causes.

Each of these points highlights how and why celebrity matters to fashion and the work that realizes and leverages celebrity. The discussion elaborates on some of Beyoncé's experimental connections with fashion as she cultivates a Forest-Beyoncé-Market. The Beyoncé phenomenon is about music and celebrity, but it is also about fashion culture. Featuring or working with Beyoncé in any manner means making or referencing particular things, many of them exploratory and cutting edge within the fashion industry. Fashion collaborations bring into relief what fashion makes and represents through texture, embodiment, and the individual and collective styles of her consumers and media fans.

21

Chapter 19: Beyoncé's Influence on Body Positivity

- All you have to do is ask: How to master the most important skill of the networked era, Fundraising when you capitalize on your community, and Equal rights for all: How to get more of what you want. We have also read and written on important topics such as agricultural labor markets, assessing learning, health services markets, and complex organizations; and have included studies that identify and provide insights on the politics behind decision making by policymakers – be they elected or not. In addition, we have included many pieces that address the activities, actions, and inactions of government and nongovernmental organizations and businesses. - In "The Beyoncé Phenomenon: From Destiny's Child to Queen Bey – Beyoncé's influence on contemporary culture, gender, and race," Jennifer C. Mueller writes about Beyoncé, a woman known for her music and on-stage performances, as well as her physical appearance and style. Jennifer C. Mueller discusses the cultural, visual, performative, and aesthetic aspects of Beyoncé's identity, and in this chapter, we look at her influence on body positivity. Professor Mueller's impressive work offers us a comprehensive analysis of Beyoncé's impact and role in reshaping beauty standards and promoting diversity in relation to body image, along with an overview of representation. "The Beyoncé Phenomenon" is an incredibly comprehensive look at a pop diva that offers many rich ideas for thinking about representations of body image.

22

Chapter 20: Beyoncé's Legacy and Future Impact

This chapter is a rare retrospective chapter which we include in this book to provide a sense of completion and of reflection for ourselves as well as for the readers. As we near the last pages of this book, we take pause to reflect on the profound impact Beyoncé has had—for anyone reading this book on the set as well as us!—as well as to mention the ways in which we think she will continue to impact the entertainment industries for years to come. Clearly we would not have undertaken this massive task of writing a 500-page manuscript were it not for our amazement for and inspiration by the one and only Queen Bey: Beyoncé.

In the end, Beyoncé is equal parts high artist and highly commercial popular entertainer. She is an icon and a jet-setting celebrity, as well as a creative force of staggering ability. While she does not rely on technology in the same way that some might, I do believe that everyone who makes music is a technologist of sorts, and Beyoncé has always been amongst the most tech-forward pop stars. In terms of humanitarian work, Beyoncé is similarly ambitious: she has long been invested in socio-political issues and the welfare of others, despite the criticisms and backlash that such actions might incur.

Whether one likes it or not, Beyoncé's further suggests the intersections between music, celebrity, and technology that continually expand in the 21st onwards. Further study will certainly be necessary: between music, between media, and then well beyond.

www.ingramcontent.com/pod-product-compliance
Lightning Source LLC
Chambersburg PA
CBHW020752150726
48196CB00023B/752